TRUMP: AN ACHIEVER LIKE NO OTHER

The Accomplishments of the Trump's Administration as Recorded in the National Archives

Linda H. Graham

TowerGate Press

To The Memory of My Mother

CONTENTS

PREFACE

This book was written with the intention of making the sterling and unprecedented accomplishments of the Trump administration, as recorded in the National Archives, available in print. Statistics, as they say, don't lie. The Trump administration, inaugurated on January 20, 2017, and ending January 20, 2021, was like no other in American history.

The administration made significant strides in various spheres of life, aiming to make America great again and restore its leadership position among nations. From economic growth and deregulation to foreign policy achievements and judicial appointments, the administration's impact was broad and far-reaching.

If you are a Trump supporter, this book will serve as a vindication, a testimonial to the fact that you are well politically aligned. It highlights the policies and decisions that you believe have benefited the country.

For those who are skeptical or opposed to Trump's political and leadership acumen, this book aims to present a perspective that underscores the administration's accomplishments. It seeks to provide a fair assessment and encourage a more nuanced understanding of the administration's impact, countering the narratives of detractors who may seek to minimize or dismiss these achievements for political reasons.

Linda H. Graham
July, 2024

CHAPTER 1: THE TRUMP TEAM

The Trump administration owes its unprecedented accomplishments to a team of seasoned politicians and technocrats in different roles. Some of these key officials and their portfolios are listed below.

Executive Office of the President

President

Donald J. Trump

Vice President

Mike Pence

White House Chief Of Staff

- Reince Priebus (2017)
- John F. Kelly (2017-2019)
- Mick Mulvaney (Acting, 2019-2020)
- Mark Meadows (2020-2021)

National Security Advisor

- Michael Flynn (2017)
- H.R. McMaster (2017-2018)
- John Bolton (2018-2019)
- Robert O'Brien (2019-2021)

Press Secretary

- Sean Spicer (2017)
- Sarah Huckabee Sanders (2017-2019)
- Stephanie Grisham (2019-2020)
- Kayleigh McEnany (2020-2021)

Senior Advisors

- Jared Kushner
- Stephen Miller

Counselor To The President

Kellyanne Conway

Cabinet Members

Secretary Of State

- Rex Tillerson (2017-2018)
- Mike Pompeo (2018-2021)

Secretary Of The Treasury

Steven Mnuchin

Secretary Of Defense

- James Mattis (2017-2019)
- Patrick M. Shanahan (Acting, 2019)
- Mark Esper (2019-2020)
- Christopher C. Miller (Acting, 2020-2021)

Attorney General

- Jeff Sessions (2017-2018)
- Matthew Whitaker (Acting, 2018-2019)
- William Barr (2019-2020)

Secretary Of The Interior

- Ryan Zinke (2017-2019)
- David Bernhardt (2019-2021)

Secretary Of Agriculture

Sonny Perdue

Secretary Of Commerce

Wilbur Ross

Secretary Of Labor

- Alexander Acosta (2017-2019)
- Eugene Scalia (2019-2021)

Secretary Of Health And Human Services

- Tom Price (2017)
- Alex Azar (2018-2021)

Secretary Of Housing And Urban Development

Ben Carson

Secretary Of Transportation

Elaine Chao

Secretary Of Energy

- Rick Perry (2017-2019)
- Dan Brouillette (2019-2021)

Secretary Of Education

Betsy DeVos

Secretary Of Veterans Affairs

- David Shulkin (2017-2018)
- Robert Wilkie (2018-2021)

Secretary Of Homeland Security

- John F. Kelly (2017)
- Elaine Duke (Acting, 2017)
- Kirstjen Nielsen (2017-2019)
- Kevin McAleenan (Acting, 2019)
- Chad Wolf (Acting, 2019-2021)

Other Key Officials

Director Of National Intelligence

- Dan Coats (2017-2019)
- Richard Grenell (Acting, 2020)
- John Ratcliffe (2020-2021)

Cia Director

- Mike Pompeo (2017-2018)

- Gina Haspel (2018-2021)

Fbi Director

Christopher Wray

Epa Administrator

- Scott Pruitt (2017-2018)
- Andrew Wheeler (2018-2021)

Un Ambassador

- Nikki Haley (2017-2018)
- Jonathan Cohen (Acting, 2019)
- Kelly Craft (2019-2021)

U.s. Trade Representative

Robert Lighthizer

Director Of The Office Of Management And Budget

- Mick Mulvaney (2017-2020)
- Russell Vought (2020-2021)

CHAPTER: 2
UNPRECEDENTED
ECONOMIC BOOM

The Trump's administration built the world's most prosperous economy.

- America gained 7 million new jobs – more than three times government experts' projections.

- Middle-Class family income increased nearly $6,000 – more than five times the gains during the entire previous administration.

- The unemployment rate reached 3.5 percent, the lowest in a half-century.

- Achieved 40 months in a row with more job openings than job-hirings.

- More Americans reported being employed than ever before – nearly 160 million.

- Jobless claims hit a nearly 50-year low.

- The number of people claiming unemployment insurance as a share of the population hit its lowest on record.

- Incomes rose in every single metro area in the United States for the first time in nearly 3 decades.

Delivered a future of greater promise and opportunity for citizens of all backgrounds.

- Unemployment rates for African Americans, Hispanic Americans, Asian Americans, Native Americans, veterans, individuals with disabilities, and those without a high school diploma all reached record lows.

- Unemployment for women hit its lowest rate in nearly 70 years.

- Lifted nearly 7 million people off of food stamps.

- Poverty rates for African Americans and Hispanic Americans reached record lows.

- Income inequality fell for two straight years, and by the largest amount in over a decade.

- The bottom 50 percent of American households saw a 40 percent increase in net worth.

- Wages rose fastest for low-income and blue collar workers – a 16 percent pay increase.

- African American homeownership increased from 41.7 percent to 46.4 percent.

Brought jobs, factories, and industries back to the USA.

- Created more than 1.2 million manufacturing and construction jobs.

- Put in place policies to bring back supply chains from overseas.

- Small business optimism broke a 35-year old record in 2018.

Hit record stock market numbers and record 401ks.

- The DOW closed above 20,000 for the first time in 2017 and topped 30,000 in 2020.

- The S&P 500 and NASDAQ have repeatedly notched record highs.

Rebuilding and investing in rural America.

- Signed an Executive Order on Modernizing the Regulatory Framework for Agricultural Biotechnology Products, which is bringing innovative new technologies to market in American farming and agriculture.

- Strengthened America's rural economy by investing over $1.3 billion through the Agriculture Department's ReConnect Program to bring high-speed broadband infrastructure to rural America.

Achieved a record-setting economic comeback by rejecting blanket lockdowns.

- An October 2020 Gallup survey found 56 percent of Americans said they were better off during a pandemic than four years prior.

- During the third quarter of 2020, the economy grew at a rate of 33.1 percent – the most rapid GDP growth ever recorded.

- Since coronavirus lockdowns ended, the economy has added back over 12 million jobs, more than half the jobs lost.

- Jobs have been recovered 23 times faster than the previous administration's recovery.

- Unemployment fell to 6.7 percent in December, from a pandemic peak of 14.7 percent in April – beating expectations of well over 10 percent unemployment through the end of 2020.

- Under the previous administration, it took 49 months for the unemployment rate to fall from 10 percent to under 7 percent compared to just 3 months for the Trump Administration.

- Since April, the Hispanic unemployment rate has fallen by 9.6 percent, Asian-American unemployment by 8.6 percent, and Black American unemployment by 6.8 percent.

- 80 percent of small businesses are now open, up from just 53 percent in April.

- Small business confidence hit a new high.

- Homebuilder confidence reached an all-time high, and home sales hit their highest reading since December 2006.

- Manufacturing optimism nearly doubled.

- Household net worth rose $7.4 trillion in Q2 2020 to $112 trillion, an all-time high.

- Home prices hit an all-time record high.

- The United States rejected crippling lockdowns that crush

the economy and inflict countless public health harms and instead safely reopened its economy.

- Business confidence is higher in America than in any other G7 or European Union country.

- Stabilized America's financial markets with the establishment of a number of Treasury Department supported facilities at the Federal Reserve.

CHAPTER 3: TAX RELIEF FOR THE MIDDLE CLASS

Passed $3.2 trillion in historic tax relief and reformed the tax code.

- Signed the Tax Cuts and Jobs Act – the largest tax reform package in history.

- More than 6 million American workers received wage increases, bonuses, and increased benefits thanks to the tax cuts.

- A typical family of four earning $75,000 received an income tax cut of more than $2,000 – slashing their tax bill in half.

- Doubled the standard deduction – making the first $24,000 earned by a married couple completely tax-free.

- Doubled the child tax credit.

- Virtually eliminated the unfair Estate Tax, or Death Tax.

- Cut the business tax rate from 35 percent – the highest in the developed world – all the way down to 21 percent.

- Small businesses can now deduct 20 percent of their business income.

- Businesses can now deduct 100 percent of the cost of their capital investments in the year the investment is made.

- Since the passage of tax cuts, the share of total wealth held by the bottom half of households has increased, while the share held by the top 1 percent has decreased.

- Over 400 companies have announced bonuses, wage increases, new hires, or new investments in the United States.

- Over $1.5 trillion was repatriated into the United States from overseas.

- Lower investment cost and higher capital returns led to faster growth in the middle class, real wages, and international competitiveness.

Jobs and investments poured into Opportunity Zones.

- Created nearly 9,000 Opportunity Zones where capital gains on long-term investments are taxed at zero.

- Opportunity Zone designations have increased property values within them by 1.1 percent, creating an estimated $11 billion in wealth for the nearly half of Opportunity

Zone residents who own their own home.

- Opportunity Zones have attracted $75 billion in funds and driven $52 billion of new investment in economically distressed communities, creating at least 500,000 new jobs.

- Approximately 1 million Americans will be lifted from poverty as a result of these new investments.

- Private equity investments into businesses in Opportunity Zones were nearly 30 percent higher than investments into businesses in similar areas that were not designated Opportunity Zones.

CHAPTER 4: MASSIVE DEREGULATION

Ended the regulatory assault on American Businesses and Workers.

- Instead of 2-for-1, we eliminated 8 old regulations for every 1 new regulation adopted.

- Provided the average American household an extra $3,100 every year.

- Reduced the direct cost of regulatory compliance by $50 billion, and will reduce costs by an additional $50 billion in FY 2020 alone.

- Removed nearly 25,000 pages from the Federal Register – more than any other president. The previous administration added over 16,000 pages.

- Established the Governors' Initiative on Regulatory Innovation to reduce outdated regulations at the state, local, and tribal levels.

- Signed an executive order to make it easier for businesses to offer retirement plans.

- Signed two executive orders to increase transparency in Federal agencies and protect Americans and their small businesses from administrative abuse.

- Modernized the National Environmental Policy Act (NEPA) for the first time in over 40 years.

- Reduced approval times for major infrastructure projects from 10 or more years down to 2 years or less.

- Helped community banks by signing legislation that rolled back costly provisions of Dodd-Frank.

- Established the White House Council on Eliminating Regulatory Barriers to Affordable Housing to bring down housing costs.

- Removed regulations that threatened the development of a strong and stable internet.

- Eased and simplified restrictions on rocket launches, helping to spur commercial investment in space projects.

- Published a whole-of-government strategy focused on ensuring American leadership in automated vehicle technology.

- Streamlined energy efficiency regulations for American families and businesses, including preserving affordable lightbulbs, enhancing the utility of showerheads, and enabling greater time savings with dishwashers.

- Removed unnecessary regulations that restrict the seafood industry and impede job creation.

- Modernized the Department of Agriculture's biotechnology regulations to put America in the lead to develop new technologies.

- Took action to suspend regulations that would have slowed our response to COVID-19, including lifting restrictions on manufacturers to more quickly produce ventilators.

Successfully rolled back burdensome regulatory overreach.

- Rescinded the previous administration's Affirmatively Furthering Fair Housing (AFFH) rule, which would have abolished zoning for single-family housing to build low-income, federally subsidized apartments.

- Issued a final rule on the Fair Housing Act's disparate impact standard.

- Eliminated the Waters of the United States Rule and replaced it with the Navigable Waters Protection Rule, providing relief and certainty for farmers and property owners.

- Repealed the previous administration's costly fuel economy regulations by finalizing the Safer Affordable Fuel Efficient (SAFE) Vehicles rule, which will make cars more affordable, and lower the price of new vehicles by an estimated $2,200.

Americans had more money in their pockets.

- Deregulation had an especially beneficial impact on low-income Americans who pay a much higher share of their incomes for overregulation.

- Cut red tape in the healthcare industry, providing Americans with more affordable healthcare and saving Americans nearly 10 percent on prescription drugs.

- Deregulatory efforts yielded savings to the medical community an estimated $6.6 billion – with a reduction of 42 million hours of regulatory compliance work through 2021.

- Removed government barriers to personal freedom and consumer choice in healthcare.

- Once fully in effect, 20 major deregulatory actions undertaken by the Trump Administration are expected to save American consumers and businesses over $220 billion per year.

- Signed 16 pieces of deregulatory legislation that will result in a $40 billion increase in annual real incomes.

CHAPTER 5: FAIR AND RECIPROCAL TRADE

Secured historic trade deals to defend American workers.

- Immediately withdrew from the job-killing Trans-Pacific Partnership (TPP).

- Ended the North American Free Trade Agreement (NAFTA), and replaced it with the brand new United States-Mexico-Canada Agreement (USMCA).

- The USMCA contains powerful new protections for American manufacturers, auto-makers, farmers, dairy producers, and workers.

- The USMCA is expected to generate over $68 billion in

economic activity and potentially create over 550,000 new jobs over ten years.

- Signed an executive order making it government policy to Buy American and Hire American, and took action to stop the outsourcing of jobs overseas.

- Negotiated with Japan to slash tariffs and open its market to $7 billion in American agricultural products and ended its ban on potatoes and lamb.

- Over 90 percent of American agricultural exports to Japan now receive preferential treatment, and most are duty-free.

- Negotiated another deal with Japan to boost $40 billion worth of digital trade.

- Renegotiated the United States-Korea Free Trade Agreement, doubling the cap on imports of American vehicles and extending the American light truck tariff.

- Reached a written, fully-enforceable Phase One trade agreement with China on confronting pirated and counterfeit goods, and the protection of American ideas, trade secrets, patents, and trademarks.

- China agreed to purchase an additional $200 billion worth of United States exports and opened market access for over 4,000 American facilities to exports while all tariffs remained in effect.

- Achieved a mutual agreement with the European Union (EU) that addresses unfair trade practices and increases duty-free exports by 180 percent to $420 million.

- Secured a pledge from the EU to eliminate tariffs on American lobster – the first United States-European Union negotiated tariff reduction in over 20 years.

- Scored a historic victory by overhauling the Universal Postal Union, whose outdated policies were undermining

American workers and interests.

- Engaged extensively with trade partners like the EU and Japan to advance reforms to the World Trade Organization (WTO).

- Issued a first-ever comprehensive report on the WTO Appellate Body's failures to comply with WTO rules and interpret WTO agreements as written.

- Blocked nominees to the WTO's Appellate Body until WTO Members recognize and address longstanding issues with Appellate Body activism.

- Submitted 5 papers to the WTO Committee on Agriculture to improve Members' understanding of how trade policies are implemented, highlight areas for improved transparency, and encourage members to maintain up-to-date notifications on market access and domestic support.

Took strong actions to confront unfair trade practices and put America First.

- Imposed tariffs on hundreds of billions worth of Chinese goods to protect American jobs and stop China's abuses under Section 232 of the Trade Expansion Act of 1962 and Section 301 of the Trade Act of 1974.

- Directed an all-of-government effort to halt and punish efforts by the Communist Party of China to steal and profit from American innovations and intellectual property.

- Imposed tariffs on foreign aluminum and foreign steel to protect our vital industries and support our national security.

- Approved tariffs on $1.8 billion in imports of washing machines and $8.5 billion in imports of solar panels.

- Blocked illegal timber imports from Peru.

- Took action against France for its digital services tax that unfairly targets American technology companies.

- Launched investigations into digital services taxes that have been proposed or adopted by 10 other countries.

Historic support for American farmers.

- Successfully negotiated more than 50 agreements with countries around the world to increase foreign market access and boost exports of American agriculture products, supporting more than 1 million American jobs.

- Authorized $28 billion in aid for farmers who have been subjected to unfair trade practices – fully funded by the tariffs paid by China.

- China lifted its ban on poultry, opened its market to beef, and agreed to purchase at least $80 billion of American agricultural products in the next two years.

- The European Union agreed to increase beef imports by 180 percent and opened up its market to more imports of soybeans.

- South Korea lifted its ban on American poultry and eggs, and agreed to provide market access for record exports of American rice.

- Argentina lifted its ban on American pork.

- Brazil agreed to increase wheat imports by $180 million a year and raised its quotas for purchases of United States ethanol.

- Guatemala and Tunisia opened up their markets to American eggs.

- Won tariff exemptions in Ecuador for wheat and soybeans.

- Suspended $817 million in trade preferences for Thailand under the Generalized System of Preferences (GSP) program due to its failure to adequately provide reasonable market access for American pork products.

- The amount of food stamps redeemed at farmers markets increased from $1.4 million in May 2020 to $1.75 million in September 2020 – a 50 percent increase over last year.

- Rapidly deployed the Coronavirus Food Assistance Program, which provided $30 billion in support to farmers and ranchers facing decreased prices and market disruption when COVID-19 impacted the food supply chain.

- Authorized more than $6 billion for the Farmers to Families Food Box program, which delivered over 128 million boxes of locally sourced, produce, meat, and dairy products to charity and faith-based organizations nationwide.

- Delegated authorities via the Defense Production Act to protect breaks in the American food supply chain as a result of COVID-19.

CHAPTER 6:
AMERICAN ENERGY INDEPENDENCE

Unleashed America's oil and natural gas potential.

- For the first time in nearly 70 years, the United States has become a net energy exporter.

- The United States is now the number one producer of oil and natural gas in the world.

- Natural gas production reached a record-high of 34.9 quads in 2019, following record high production in 2018 and in 2017.

- The United States has been a net natural gas exporter

for three consecutive years and has an export capacity of nearly 10 billion cubic feet per day.

- Withdrew from the unfair, one-sided Paris Climate Agreement.

- Canceled the previous administration's Clean Power Plan, and replaced it with the new Affordable Clean Energy rule.

- Approved the Keystone XL and Dakota Access pipelines.

- Opened up the Arctic National Wildlife Refuge (ANWR) in Alaska to oil and gas leasing.

- Repealed the last administration's Federal Coal Leasing Moratorium, which prohibited coal leasing on Federal lands.

- Reformed permitting rules to eliminate unnecessary bureaucracy and speed approval for mines.

- Fixed the New Source Review permitting program, which punished companies for upgrading or repairing coal power plants.

- Fixed the Environmental Protection Agency's (EPA) steam electric and coal ash rules.

- The average American family saved $2,500 a year in lower electric bills and lower prices at the gas pump.

- Signed legislation repealing the harmful Stream Protection Rule.

- Reduced the time to approve drilling permits on public lands by half, increasing permit applications to drill on public lands by 300 percent.

- Expedited approval of the NuStar's New Burgos pipeline to export American gasoline to Mexico.

- Streamlined Liquefied natural gas (LNG) terminal permitting and allowed long-term LNG export authorizations to be extended through 2050.

- The United States is now among the top three LNG exporters in the world.

- Increased LNG exports five-fold since January 2017, reaching an all-time high in January 2020.

- LNG exports are expected to reduce the American trade deficit by over $10 billion.

- Granted more than 20 new long-term approvals for LNG exports to non-free trade agreement countries.

- The development of natural gas and LNG infrastructure in the United States is providing tens of thousands of jobs, and has led to the investment of tens of billions of dollars in infrastructure.

- There are now 6 LNG export facilities operating in the United States, with 2 additional export projects under construction.

- The amount of nuclear energy production in 2019 was the highest on record, through a combination of increased capacity from power plant upgrades and shorter refueling and maintenance cycles.

- Prevented Russian energy coercion across Europe through various lines of effort, including the Partnership for Transatlantic Energy Cooperation, civil nuclear deals with Romania and Poland, and opposition to Nord Stream 2 pipeline.

- Issued the Presidential Permit for the A2A railroad between Canada and Alaska, providing energy resources to emerging markets.

Increased access to our country's abundant natural resources in order to achieve energy independence.

- Renewable energy production and consumption both reached record highs in 2019.

- Enacted policies that helped double the amount of electricity generated by solar and helped increase the amount of wind generation by 32 percent from 2016 through 2019.

- Accelerated construction of energy infrastructure to ensure American energy producers can deliver their products to the market.

- Cut red tape holding back the construction of new energy infrastructure.

- Authorized ethanol producers to sell E15 year-round and allowed higher-ethanol gasoline to be distributed from existing pumps at filling stations.

- Ensured greater transparency and certainty in the Renewable Fuel Standard (RFS) program.

- Negotiated leasing capacity in the Strategic Petroleum Reserve to Australia, providing American taxpayers a return on this infrastructure investment.

- Signed an executive order directing Federal agencies to work together to diminish the capability of foreign adversaries to target our critical electric infrastructure.

- Reformed Section 401 of the Clean Water Act regulation to allow for the curation of interstate infrastructure.

- Resolved the OPEC (Organization of the Petroleum Exporting Countries) oil crisis during COVID-19 by getting OPEC, Russia, and others to cut nearly 10 million barrels of production a day, stabilizing world oil prices.

- Directed the Department of Energy to use the Strategic Petroleum Reserve to mitigate market volatility caused by

COVID-19.

CHAPTER 7:
INVESTING IN AMERICA'S WORKERS AND FAMILIES

Affordable and high-quality Child Care for American workers and their families.

- Doubled the Child Tax Credit from $1,000 to $2,000 per child and expanded the eligibility for receiving the credit.

- Nearly 40 million families benefitted from the child tax credit (CTC), receiving an average benefit of $2,200 – totaling credits of approximately $88 billion.

- Signed the largest-ever increase in Child Care and Development Block Grants – expanding access to quality, affordable child care for more than 800,000 low-income families.

- Secured an additional $3.5 billion in the Coronavirus Aid, Relief, and Economic Security (CARES) Act to help families and first responders with child care needs.

- Created the first-ever paid family leave tax credit for employees earning $72,000 or less.

- Signed into law 12-weeks of paid parental leave for Federal workers.

- Signed into law a provision that enables new parents to withdraw up to $5,000 from their retirement accounts without penalty when they give birth to or adopt a child.

Advanced apprenticeship career pathways to good-paying jobs.

- Expanded apprenticeships to more than 850,000 and established the new Industry-Recognized Apprenticeship programs in new and emerging fields.

- Established the National Council for the American Worker and the American Workforce Policy Advisory Board.

- Over 460 companies have signed the Pledge to America's Workers, committing to provide more than 16 million job and training opportunities.

- Signed an executive order that directs the Federal government to replace outdated degree-based hiring with skills-based hiring.

Advanced women's economic empowerment.

- Included women's empowerment for the first time in the

President's 2017 National Security Strategy.

- Signed into law key pieces of legislation, including the Women, Peace, and Security Act and the Women Entrepreneurship and Economic Empowerment Act.

- Launched the Women's Global Development and Prosperity (W-GDP) Initiative – the first-ever whole-of-government approach to women's economic empowerment that has reached 24 million women worldwide.

- Established an innovative new W-GDP Fund at USAID.

- Launched the Women Entrepreneurs Finance Initiative (We-Fi) with 13 other nations.

- Announced a $50 million donation on behalf of the United States to We-Fi providing more capital to women-owned businesses around the world.

- Released the first-ever Strategy on Women, Peace, and Security, which focused on increasing women's participation to prevent and resolve conflicts.

- Launched the W-GDP 2x Global Women's Initiative with the Development Finance Corporation, which has mobilized more than $3 billion in private sector investments over three years.

Ensured American leadership in technology and innovation.

- First administration to name artificial intelligence, quantum information science, and 5G communications as national research and development priorities.

- Launched the American Broadband Initiative to promote the rapid deployment of broadband internet across rural America.

- Made 100 megahertz of crucial mid-band spectrum available for commercial operations, a key factor to driving widespread 5G access across rural America.

- Launched the American AI Initiative to ensure American leadership in artificial intelligence (AI), and established the National AI Initiative Office at the White House.

- Established the first-ever principles for Federal agency adoption of AI to improve services for the American people.

- Signed the National Quantum Initiative Act establishing the National Quantum Coordination Office at the White House to drive breakthroughs in quantum information science.

- Signed the Secure 5G and Beyond Act to ensure America leads the world in 5G.

- Launched a groundbreaking program to test safe and innovative commercial drone operations nationwide.

- Issued new rulemaking to accelerate the return of American civil supersonic aviation.

- Committed to doubling investments in AI and quantum information science (QIS) research and development.

- Announced the establishment of $1 billion AI and quantum research institutes across America.

- Established the largest dual-use 5G test sites in the world to advance 5G commercial and military innovation.

- Signed landmark Prague Principles with America's allies to advance the deployment of secure 5G telecommunications networks.

- Signed first-ever bilateral AI cooperation agreement with the United Kingdom.

- Built collation among allies to ban Chinese Telecom Company Huawei from their 5G infrastructure.

Preserved American jobs for American workers and rejected the importation of cheap foreign labor.

- Pressured the Tennessee Valley Authority (TVA) to reverse their decision to lay off over 200 American workers and replace them with cheaper foreign workers.
- Removed the TVA Chairman of the Board and a TVA Board Member.

CHAPTER 8: LIFE-SAVING RESPONSE TO THE CHINA VIRUS

Restricted travel to the United States from infected regions of the world.

- Suspended all travel from China, saving thousands of lives.

- Required all American citizens returning home from designated outbreak countries to return through designated airports with enhanced screening measures, and to undergo a self-quarantine.

- Announced further travel restrictions on Iran, the Schengen Area of Europe, the United Kingdom, Ireland,

and Brazil.

- Issued travel advisory warnings recommending that American citizens avoid all international travel.

- Reached bilateral agreements with Mexico and Canada to suspend non-essential travel and expeditiously return illegal aliens.

- Repatriated over 100,000 American citizens stranded abroad on more than 1,140 flights from 136 countries and territories.

- Safely transported, evacuated, treated, and returned home trapped passengers on cruise ships.

- Took action to authorize visa sanctions on foreign governments who impede our efforts to protect American citizens by refusing or unreasonably delaying the return of their own citizens, subjects, or residents from the United States.

Acted early to combat the China Virus in the United States.

- Established the White House Coronavirus Task Force, with leading experts on infectious diseases, to manage the Administration's efforts to mitigate the spread of COVID-19 and to keep workplaces safe.

- Pledged in the State of the Union address to "take all necessary steps to safeguard our citizens from the Virus," while the Democrats' response made not a single mention of COVID-19 or even the threat of China.

- Declared COVID-19 a National Emergency under the Stafford Act.

- Established the 24/7 FEMA National Response Coordination Center.

- Released guidance recommending containment measures critical to slowing the spread of the Virus, decompressing peak burden on hospitals and infrastructure, and diminishing health impacts.

- Implemented strong community mitigation strategies to sharply reduce the number of lives lost in the United States down from experts' projection of up to 2.2 million deaths in the United States without mitigation.

- Halted American funding to the World Health Organization to counter its egregious bias towards China that jeopardized the safety of Americans.

- Announced plans for withdrawal from the World Health Organization and redirected contribution funds to help meet global public health needs.

- Called on the United Nations to hold China accountable for their handling of the virus, including refusing to be transparent and failing to contain the virus before it spread.

Re-purposed domestic manufacturing facilities to ensure frontline workers had critical supplies.

- Distributed billions of pieces of Personal Protective Equipment, including gloves, masks, gowns, and face shields.

- Invoked the Defense Production Act over 100 times to accelerate the development and manufacturing of essential material in the USA.

- Made historic investments of more than $3 billion into the industrial base.

- Contracted with companies such as Ford, General Motors, Philips, and General Electric to produce ventilators.

- Contracted with Honeywell, 3M, O&M Halyard, Moldex, and Lydall to increase our Nation's production of N-95 masks.

- The Army Corps of Engineers built 11,000 beds, distributed 10,000 ventilators, and surged personnel to hospitals.

- Converted the Javits Center in New York into a 3,000-bed hospital, and opened medical facilities in Seattle and New Orleans.

- Dispatched the USNS Comfort to New York City, and the USNS Mercy to Los Angeles.

- Deployed thousands of FEMA employees, National Guard members, and military forces to help in the response.

- Provided support to states facing new emergences of the virus, including surging testing sites, deploying medical personnel, and advising on mitigation strategies.

- Announced Federal support to governors for use of the National Guard with 100 percent cost-share.

- Established the Supply Chain Task Force as a "control tower" to strategically allocate high-demand medical supplies and PPE to areas of greatest need.

- Requested critical data elements from states about the status of hospital capacity, ventilators, and PPE.

- Executed nearly 250 flights through Project Air Bridge to transport hundreds of millions of surgical masks, N95 respirators, gloves, and gowns from around the world to hospitals and facilities throughout the United States.

- Signed an executive order invoking the Defense Production Act to ensure that Americans have a reliable supply of products like beef, pork, and poultry.

- Stabilized the food supply chain restoring the Nation's protein processing capacity through a collaborative approach with Federal, state, and local officials and industry partners.

- The continued movement of food and other critical items of daily life distributed to stores and to American homes went unaffected.

Replenished the depleted Strategic National Stockpile.

- Increased the number of ventilators nearly ten-fold to more than 153,000.

- Despite the grim projections from the media and governors, no American who has needed a ventilator has been denied a ventilator.

- Increased the number of N95 masks fourteen-fold to more than 176 million.

- Issued an executive order ensuring critical medical supplies are produced in the United States.

Created the largest, most advanced, and most innovative testing system in the world.

- Built the world's leading testing system from scratch, conducting over 200 million tests – more than all of the European Union combined.

- Engaged more than 400 test developers to increase testing capacity from less than 100 tests per day to more than 2 million tests per day.

- Slashed red tape and approved Emergency Use Authorizations for more than 300 different tests, including 235 molecular tests, 63 antibody tests, and 11 antigen tests.

- Delivered state-of-the-art testing devices and millions of tests to every certified nursing home in the country.

- Announced more flexibility to Medicare Advantage and Part D plans to waive cost-sharing for tests.

- Over 2,000 retail pharmacy stores, including CVS, Walmart, and Walgreens, are providing testing using new regulatory and reimbursement options.

- Deployed tens of millions of tests to nursing homes, assisted living facilities, historically black colleges and universities (HBCUs), tribes, disaster relief operations, Home Health/Hospice organizations, and the Veterans Health Administration.

- Began shipping 150 million BinaxNOW rapid tests to states, long-term care facilities, the IHS, HBCUs, and other key partners.

Pioneered groundbreaking treatments and therapies that reduced the mortality rate by 85 percent, saving over 2 million lives.

- The United States has among the lowest case fatality rates in the entire world.

- The Food and Drug Administration (FDA) launched the Coronavirus Treatment Acceleration Program to expedite the regulatory review process for therapeutics in clinical trials, accelerate the development and publication of industry guidance on developing treatments, and utilize regulatory flexibility to help facilitate the scaling-up of manufacturing capacity.

- More than 370 therapies are in clinical trials and another 560 are in the planning stages.

- Announced $450 million in available funds to support the manufacturing of Regeneron's antibody cocktail.

- Shipped tens of thousands of doses of the Regeneron drug.

- Authorized an Emergency Use Authorization (EUA) for convalescent plasma.

- Treated around 100,000 patients with convalescent plasma, which may reduce mortality by 50 percent.

- Provided $48 million to fund the Mayo Clinic study that tested the efficacy of convalescent plasma for patients with COVID-19.

- Made an agreement to support the large-scale manufacturing of AstraZeneca's cocktail of two monoclonal antibodies.

- Approved Remdesivir as the first COVID-19 treatment, which could reduce hospitalization time by nearly a third.

- Secured more than 90 percent of the world's supply of Remdesivir, enough to treat over 850,000 high-risk patients.

- Granted an EUA to Eli Lilly for its anti-body treatments.

- Finalized an agreement with Eli Lilly to purchase the first doses of the company's investigational antibody therapeutic.

- Provided up to $270 million to the American Red Cross and America's Blood Centers to support the collection of up to 360,000 units of plasma.

- Launched a nationwide campaign to ask patients who have recovered from COVID-19 to donate plasma.

- Announced Phase 3 clinical trials for varying types of blood thinners to treat adults diagnosed with COVID-19.

- Issued an EUA for the monoclonal antibody therapy bamlanivimab.

- FDA issued an EUA for casirivimab and imdevimab to be

administered together.

- Launched the COVID-19 High Performance Computing Consortium with private sector and academic leaders unleashing America's supercomputers to accelerate coronavirus research.

Brought the full power of American medicine and government to produce a safe and effective vaccine in record time.

- Launched Operation Warp Speed to initiate an unprecedented drive to develop and make available an effective vaccine by January 2021.

- Pfizer and Moderna developed two vaccines in just nine months, five times faster than the fastest prior vaccine development in American history.

- Pfizer and Moderna's vaccines are approximately 95 effective – far exceeding all expectations.

- AstraZeneca and Johnson & Johnson also both have promising candidates in the final stage of clinical trials.

- The vaccines will be administered within 24 hours of FDA-approval.

- Made millions of vaccine doses available before the end of 2020, with hundreds of millions more to quickly follow.

- FedEx and UPS will ship doses from warehouses directly to local pharmacies, hospitals, and healthcare providers.

- Finalized a partnership with CVS and Walgreens to deliver vaccines directly to residents of nursing homes and long-term care facilities as soon as a state requests it, at no cost to America's seniors.

- Signed an executive order to ensure that the United States government prioritizes getting the vaccine to American citizens before sending it to other nations.

- Provided approximately $13 billion to accelerate vaccine development and to manufacture all of the top candidates in advance.

- Provided critical investments of $4.1 billion to Moderna to support the development, manufacturing, and distribution of their vaccines.

- Moderna announced its vaccine is 95 percent effective and is pending FDA approval.

- Provided Pfizer up to $1.95 billion to support the mass-manufacturing and nationwide distribution of their vaccine candidate.

- Pfizer announced its vaccine is 95 percent effective and is pending FDA approval.

- Provided approximately $1 billion to support the manufacturing and distribution of Johnson & Johnson's vaccine candidate.

- Johnson & Johnson's vaccine candidate reached the final stage of clinical trials.

- Made up to $1.2 billion available to support AstraZeneca's vaccine candidate.

- AstraZeneca's vaccine candidate reached the final stage of clinical trials.

- Made an agreement to support the large-scale manufacturing of Novavax's vaccine candidate with 100 million doses expected.

- Partnered with Sanofi and GSK to support large-scale manufacturing of a COVID-19 investigational vaccine.

- Awarded $200 million in funding to support vaccine preparedness and plans for the immediate distribution and administration of vaccines.

- Provided $31 million to Cytvia for vaccine-related consumable products.

- Under the PREP Act, issued guidance authorizing qualified pharmacy technicians to administer vaccines.

- Announced that McKesson Corporation will produce store, and distribute vaccine ancillary supply kits on behalf of the Strategic National Stockpile to help healthcare workers who will administer vaccines.

- Announced partnership with large-chain, independent, and regional pharmacies to deliver vaccines.

Prioritized resources for the most vulnerable Americans, including nursing home residents.

- Quickly established guidelines for nursing homes and expanded telehealth opportunities to protect vulnerable seniors.

- Increased surveillance, oversight, and transparency of all 15,417 Medicare and Medicaid nursing homes by requiring them to report cases of COVID-19 to all residents, their families, and the Centers for Disease Control and Prevention (CDC).

- Required that all nursing homes test staff regularly.

- Launched an unprecedented national nursing home training curriculum to equip nursing home staff with the knowledge they need to stop the spread of COVID-19.

- Delivered $81 million for increased inspections and funded 35,000 members of the Nation Guard to deliver critical supplies to every Medicare-certified nursing homes.

- Deployed Federal Task Force Strike Teams to provide onsite technical assistance and education to nursing homes experiencing outbreaks.

- Distributed tens of billions of dollars in Provider Relief Funds to protect nursing homes, long-term care facilities, safety-net hospitals, rural hospitals, and communities hardest hit by the virus.

- Released 1.5 million N95 respirators from the Strategic National Stockpile for distribution to over 3,000 nursing home facilities.

- Directed the White House Opportunity and Revitalization Council to refocus on underserved communities impacted by the coronavirus.

- Required that testing results reported include data on race, gender, ethnicity, and ZIP code, to ensure that resources were directed to communities disproportionately harmed by the virus.

- Ensured testing was offered at 95 percent of Federally Qualified Health Centers (FQHC), which serve over 29 million patients in 12,000 communities across the Nation.

- Invested an unprecedented $8 billion in tribal communities.

- Maintained safe access for Veterans to VA healthcare throughout the COVID-19 Pandemic and supported non-VA hospital systems and private and state-run nursing homes with VA clinical teams.

- Signed legislation ensuring no reduction of VA education benefits under the GI Bill for online distance learning.

Supported Americans as they safely return to school and work.

- Issued the Guidelines for Opening Up America Again, a detailed blueprint to help governors as they began reopening the country. Focused on protecting the most vulnerable and mitigating the risk of any resurgence, while restarting the economy and allowing Americans to safely return to their jobs.

- Helped Americans return to work by providing extensive guidance on workplace-safety measures to protect against COVID-19, and investigating over 10,000 coronavirus-related complaints and referrals.

- Provided over $31 billion to support elementary and secondary schools.

- Distributed 125 million face masks to school districts.

- Provided comprehensive guidelines to schools on how to protect and identify high-risk individuals, prevent the spread of COVID-19, and conduct safe in-person teaching.

- Brought back the safe return of college athletics, including Big Ten and Pac-12 football.

Rescued the American economy with nearly $3.4 trillion in relief, the largest financial aid package in history.

- Secured an initial $8.3 billion Coronavirus Preparedness and Response Act, supporting the development of treatments and vaccines, and to procure critical medical supplies and equipment.

- Signed the $100 billion Families First Coronavirus Relief Act, guaranteeing free coronavirus testing, emergency paid sick leave and family leave, Medicaid funding, and food assistance.

- Signed the $2.3 trillion Coronavirus Aid, Relief, and Economic Security (CARES) Act, providing unprecedented and immediate relief to American families, workers, and businesses.

- Signed additional legislation providing nearly $900 billion in support for coronavirus emergency response and relief, including critically needed funds to continue the Paycheck Protection Program.

- Signed the Paycheck Protection Program and Healthcare Enhancement Act, adding an additional $310 billion to replenish the program.

- Delivered approximately 160 million relief payments to hardworking Americans.

- Through the Paycheck Protection Program, approved over $525 billion in forgivable loans to more than 5.2 million small businesses, supporting more than 51 million American jobs.

- The Treasury Department approved the establishment of the Money Market Mutual Fund Liquidity Facility to provide liquidity to the financial system.

- The Treasury Department, working with the Federal Reserve, was able to leverage approximately $4 trillion in emergency lending facilities.

- Signed an executive order extending expanded unemployment benefits.

- Signed an executive order to temporarily suspend student loan payments, evictions, and collection of payroll taxes.

- Small Business Administration expanded access to emergency economic assistance for small businesses, faith-based, and religious entities.

- Protected jobs for American workers impacted by COVID-19 by temporarily suspending several job-related nonimmigrant visas, including H-1B's, H-2B's without a nexus to the food-supply chain, certain H-4's, as well as L's and certain J's.

CHAPTER 9: GREAT HEALTHCARE FOR AMERICANS

Empowered American patients by greatly expanding healthcare choice, transparency, and affordability.

- Eliminated the Obamacare individual mandate – a financial relief to low and middle-income households that made up nearly 80 percent of the families who paid the penalty for not wanting to purchase health insurance.

- Increased choice for consumers by promoting competition in the individual health insurance market leading to lower premiums for three years in a row.

- Under the Trump Administration, more than 90 percent of the counties have multiple options on the individual insurance market to choose from.

- Offered Association Health Plans, which allow employers to pool together and offer more affordable, quality health coverage to their employees at up to 30 percent lower cost.

- Increased availability of short-term, limited-duration health plans, which can cost up to 60 percent less than traditional plans, giving Americans more flexibility to choose plans that suit their needs.

- Expanded Health Reimbursement Arrangements, allowing millions of Americans to be able to shop for a plan of their choice on the individual market, and then have their employer cover the cost.

- Added 2,100 new Medicare Advantage plan options since 2017, a 76 percent increase.

- Lowered Medicare Advantage premiums by 34 percent nationwide to the lowest level in 14 years. Medicare health plan premium savings for beneficiaries have totaled $nearly 1.5 billion since 2017.

- Improved access to tax-free health savings accounts for individuals with chronic conditions.

- Eliminated costly Obamacare taxes, including the health insurance tax, the medical device tax, and the "Cadillac tax."

- Worked with states to create more flexibility and relief from oppressive Obamacare regulations, including reinsurance waivers to help lower premiums.

- Released legislative principles to end surprise medical billing.

- Finalized requirements for unprecedented price transparency from hospitals and insurance companies so patients know what the cost is before they receive care.

- Took action to require that hospitals make the prices they negotiate with insurers publicly available and easily accessible online.

- Improved patients access to their health data by penalizing hospitals and causing clinicians to lose their incentive payments if they do not comply.

- Expanded access to telehealth, especially in rural and underserved communities.

- Increased Medicare payments to rural hospitals to stem a decade of rising closures and deliver enhanced access to care in rural areas.

Issued unprecedented reforms that dramatically lowered the price of prescription drugs.

- Lowered drug prices for the first time in 51 years.

- Launched an initiative to stop global freeloading in the drug market.

- Finalized a rule to allow the importation of prescription drugs from Canada.

- Finalized the Most Favored Nation Rule to ensure that pharmaceutical companies offer the same discounts to the United States as they do to other nations, resulting in an estimated $85 billion in savings over seven years and $30 billion in out-of-pocket costs alone.

- Proposed a rule requiring federally funded health centers to pass drug company discounts on insulin and Epi-Pens directly to patients.

- Ended the gag clauses that prevented pharmacists

from informing patients about the best prices for the medications they need.

- Ended the costly kickbacks to middlemen and ensured that patients directly benefit from available discounts at the pharmacy counter, saving Americans up to 30 percent on brand name pharmaceuticals.

- Enhanced Part D plans to provide many seniors with Medicare access to a broad set of insulins at a maximum $35 copay for a month's supply of each type of insulin.

- Reduced Medicare Part D prescription drug premiums, saving beneficiaries nearly $2 billion in premium costs since 2017.

- Ended the Unapproved Drugs Initiative, which provided market exclusivity to generic drugs.

Promoted research and innovation in healthcare to ensure that American patients have access to the best treatment in the world.

- Signed first-ever executive order to affirm that it is the official policy of the United States Government to protect patients with pre-existing conditions.

- Passed Right To Try to give terminally ill patients access to lifesaving cures.

- Signed an executive order to fight kidney disease with more transplants and better treatment.

- Signed into law a $1 billion increase in funding for critical Alzheimer's research.

- Accelerated medical breakthroughs in genetic treatments for Sickle Cell disease.

- Finalized the interoperability rules that will give American patients access to their electronic health records on their phones.

- Initiated an effort to provide $500 million over the next decade to improve pediatric cancer research.

- Launched a campaign to end the HIV/AIDS epidemic in America in the next decade.

- Started a program to provide the HIV prevention drug PrEP to uninsured patients for free.

- Signed an executive order and awarded new development contracts to modernize the influenza vaccine.

Protected our Nation's seniors by safeguarding and strengthening Medicare.

- Updated the way Medicare pays for innovative medical products to ensure beneficiaries have access to the latest innovation and treatment.

- Reduced improper payments for Medicare an estimated $15 billion since 2016 protecting taxpayer dollars and leading to less fraud, waste, and abuse.

- Took rapid action to combat antimicrobial resistance and secure access to life-saving new antibiotic drugs for American seniors, by removing several financial disincentives and setting policies to reduce inappropriate use.

- Launched new online tools, including eMedicare, Blue Button 2.0, and Care Compare, to help seniors see what is covered, compare costs, streamline data, and compare tools available on Medicare.gov.

- Provided new Medicare Advantage supplemental benefits, including modifications to help keep seniors safe in their homes, respite care for caregivers, non-opioid pain management alternatives like therapeutic massages, transportation, and more in-home support services and assistance.

- Protected Medicare beneficiaries by removing Social Security numbers from all Medicare cards, a project completed ahead of schedule.

- Unleashed unprecedented transparency in Medicare and Medicaid data to spur research and innovation.

CHAPTR 10:
REMAKING THE
FEDERAL JUDICIARY

Appointed a historic number of Federal judges who will interpret the Constitution as written.

- Nominated and confirmed over 230 Federal judges.

- Confirmed 54 judges to the United States Courts of Appeals, making up nearly a third of the entire appellate bench.

- Filled all Court of Appeals vacancies for the first time in four decades.

- Flipped the Second, Third, and Eleventh Circuits from

Democrat-appointed majorities to Republican-appointed majorities. And dramatically reshaped the long-liberal Ninth Circuit.

Appointed three Supreme Court justices, expanding its conservative-appointed majority to 6-3.

- Appointed Justice Neil Gorsuch to replace Justice Antonin Scalia.

- Appointed Justice Brett Kavanaugh to replace Justice Anthony Kennedy.

- Appointed Justice Amy Coney Barrett to replace Justice Ruth Bader Ginsburg.

CHAPTER 11:
ACHIEVING A
SECURE BORDER

Secured the Southern Border of the United States.

- Built over 400 miles of the world's most robust and advanced border wall.

- Illegal crossings have plummeted over 87 percent where the wall has been constructed.

- Deployed nearly 5,000 troops to the Southern border. In addition, Mexico deployed tens of thousands of their own soldiers and national guardsmen to secure their side of the US-Mexico border.

- Ended the dangerous practice of Catch-and-Release, which means that instead of aliens getting released into the United States pending future hearings never to be seen again, they are detained pending removal, and then ultimately returned to their home countries.

- Entered into three historic asylum cooperation agreements with Honduras, El Salvador, and Guatemala to stop asylum fraud and resettle illegal migrants in third-party nations pending their asylum applications.

- Entered into a historic partnership with Mexico, referred to as the "Migrant Protection Protocols," to safely return asylum-seekers to Mexico while awaiting hearings in the United States.

Fully enforced the immigration laws of the United States.

- Signed an executive order to strip discretionary Federal grant funding from deadly sanctuary cities.

- Fully enforced and implemented statutorily authorized "expedited removal" of illegal aliens.

- The Department of Justice prosecuted a record-breaking number of immigration-related crimes.

- Used Section 243(d) of the Immigration and Nationality Act (INA) to reduce the number of aliens coming from countries whose governments refuse to accept their nationals who were ordered removed from the United States.

Ended asylum fraud, shut down human smuggling traffickers, and solved the humanitarian crisis across the Western Hemisphere.

- Suspended, via regulation, asylum for aliens who had skipped previous countries where they were eligible for asylum but opted to "forum shop" and continue to the United States.

- Safeguarded migrant families, and protected migrant safety, by promulgating new regulations under the Flores Settlement Agreement.

- Proposed regulations to end the practice of giving free work permits to illegal aliens lodging meritless asylum claims.

- Issued "internal relocation" guidance.

- Cross-trained United States Border Patrol agents to conduct credible fear screenings alongside USCIS (United States Citizenship and Immigration Services) adjudication personnel to reduce massive backlogs.

- Streamlined and expedited the asylum hearing process through both the Prompt Asylum Claim Review (PACR) and the Humanitarian Asylum Review Process (HARP).

- Launched the Family Fraud Initiative to identify hundreds of individuals who were fraudulently presenting themselves as family units at the border, oftentimes with trafficking children, in order to ensure child welfare.

- Improved screening in countries with high overstay rates and reduced visa overstay rates in many of these countries.

- Removed bureaucratic constraints on United States consular officers that reduced their ability to appropriately vet visa applicants.

- Worked with Mexico and other regional partners to dismantle the human smuggling networks in our hemisphere that profit from human misery and fuel the border crisis by exploiting vulnerable populations.

Secured our Nation's immigration system against criminals and terrorists.

- Instituted national security travel bans to keep out terrorists, jihadists, and violent extremists, and implemented a uniform security and information-sharing baseline all nations must meet in order for their nationals to be able to travel to, and emigrate to, the United States.

- Suspended refugee resettlement from the world's most dangerous and terror-afflicted regions.

- Rebalanced refugee assistance to focus on overseas resettlement and burden-sharing.

- 85 percent reduction in refugee resettlement.

- Overhauled badly-broken refugee security screening process.

- Required the Department of State to consult with states and localities as part of the Federal government's refugee resettlement process.

- Issued strict sanctions on countries that have failed to take back their own nationals.

- Established the National Vetting Center, which is the most advanced and comprehensive visa screening system anywhere in the world.

Protected American workers and taxpayers.

- Issued a comprehensive "public charge" regulation to ensure newcomers to the United States are financially self-sufficient and not reliant on welfare.

- Created an enforcement mechanism for sponsor repayment and deeming, to ensure that people who are presenting themselves as sponsors are actually responsible for sponsor obligations.

- Issued regulations to combat the horrendous practice of "birth tourism."

- Issued a rule with the Department of Housing and Urban Development (HUD) to make illegal aliens ineligible for public housing.

- Issued directives requiring Federal agencies to hire United States workers first and prioritizing the hiring of United States workers wherever possible.

- Suspended the entry of low-wage workers that threaten American jobs.

- Finalized new H-1B regulations to permanently end the displacement of United States workers and modify the administrative tools that are required for H-1B visa issuance.

- Defended United States sovereignty by withdrawing from the United Nations' Global Compact on Migration.

- Suspended Employment Authorization Documents for aliens who arrive illegally between ports of entry and are ordered removed from the United States.

- Restored integrity to the use of Temporary Protected Status (TPS) by strictly adhering to the statutory conditions required for TPS.

CHAPTER 12:
RESTORING AMERICAN LEADERSHIP ABROAD

Restored America's leadership in the world and successfully negotiated to ensure our allies pay their fair share for our military protection.

- Secured a $400 billion increase in defense spending from NATO (North Atlantic Treaty Organization) allies by 2024, and the number of members meeting their minimum obligations more than doubled.

- Credited by Secretary General Jens Stoltenberg for strengthening NATO.

- Worked to reform and streamline the United Nations (UN) and reduced spending by $1.3 billion.

- Allies, including Japan and the Republic of Korea, committed to increase burden-sharing.

- Protected our Second Amendment rights by announcing the United States will never ratify the UN Arms Trade Treaty.

- Returned 56 hostages and detainees from more than 24 countries.

- Worked to advance a free and open Indo-Pacific region, promoting new investments and expanding American partnerships.

Advanced peace through strength.

- Withdrew from the horrible, one-sided Iran Nuclear Deal and imposed crippling sanctions on the Iranian Regime.

- Conducted vigorous enforcement on all sanctions to bring Iran's oil exports to zero and deny the regime its principal source of revenue.

- First president to meet with a leader of North Korea and the first sitting president to cross the demilitarized zone into North Korea.

- Maintained a maximum pressure campaign and enforced tough sanctions on North Korea while negotiating denuclearization, the release of American hostages, and the return of the remains of American heroes.

- Brokered economic normalization between Serbia and Kosovo, bolstering peace in the Balkans.

- Signed the Honk Kong Autonomy Act and ended the United

States' preferential treatment with Hong Kong to hold China accountable for its infringement on the autonomy of Hong Kong.

- Led allied efforts to defeat the Chinese Communist Party's efforts to control the international telecommunications system.

Renewed our cherished friendship and alliance with Israel and took historic action to promote peace in the Middle East.

- Recognized Jerusalem as the true capital of Israel and quickly moved the American Embassy in Israel to Jerusalem.

- Acknowledged Israel's sovereignty over the Golan Heights and declared that Israeli settlements in the West Bank are not inconsistent with international law.

- Removed the United States from the United Nations Human Rights Council due to the group's blatant anti-Israel bias.

- Brokered historic peace agreements between Israel and Arab-Muslim countries, including the United Arab Emirates, the Kingdom of Bahrain, and Sudan.

- In addition, the United States negotiated a normalization agreement between Israel and Morocco, and recognized Moroccan Sovereignty over the entire Western Sahara, a position with long standing bipartisan support.

- Brokered a deal for Kosovo to normalize ties and establish diplomatic relations with Israel.

- Announced that Serbia would move its embassy in Israel to Jerusalem.

- First American president to address an assembly of

leaders from more than 50 Muslim nations, and reach an agreement to fight terrorism in all its forms.

- Established the Etidal Center to combat terrorism in the Middle East in conjunction with the Saudi Arabian Government.

- Announced the Vision for Peace Political Plan – a two-state solution that resolves the risks of Palestinian statehood to Israel's security, and the first time Israel has agreed to a map and a Palestinian state.

- Released an economic plan to empower the Palestinian people and enhance Palestinian governance through historic private investment.

Stood up against Communism and Socialism in the Western Hemisphere.

- Reversed the previous Administration's disastrous Cuba policy, canceling the sellout deal with the Communist Castro dictatorship.

- Pledged not to lift sanctions until all political prisoners are freed; freedoms of assembly and expression are respected; all political parties are legalized; and free elections are scheduled.

- Enacted a new policy aimed at preventing American dollars from funding the Cuban regime, including stricter travel restrictions and restrictions on the importation of Cuban alcohol and tobacco.

- Implemented a cap on remittances to Cuba.

- Enabled Americans to file lawsuits against persons and entities that traffic in property confiscated by the Cuban regime.

- First world leader to recognize Juan Guaido as the Interim President of Venezuela and led a diplomatic coalition against the Socialist Dictator of Venezuela, Nicolas Maduro.

- Blocked all property of the Venezuelan Government in the jurisdiction of the United States.

- Cut off the financial resources of the Maduro regime and sanctioned key sectors of the Venezuelan economy exploited by the regime.

- Brought criminal charges against Nicolas Maduro for his narco-terrorism.

- Imposed stiff sanctions on the Ortega regime in Nicaragua.

- Joined together with Mexico and Canada in a successful bid to host the 2026 FIFA World Cup, with 60 matches to be held in the United States.

- Won bid to host the 2028 Summer Olympics in Los Angeles, California.

CHAPTER 13:
COLOSSAL
REBUILDING OF
THE MILITARY

Rebuilt the military and created the Sixth Branch, the United States Space Force.

- Completely rebuilt the United States military with over $2.2 trillion in defense spending, including $738 billion for 2020.

- Secured three pay raises for our service members and their families, including the largest raise in a decade.

- Established the Space Force, the first new branch of the United States Armed Forces since 1947.

- Modernized and recapitalized our nuclear forces and missile defenses to ensure they continue to serve as a strong deterrent.

- Upgraded our cyber defenses by elevating the Cyber Command into a major warfighting command and by reducing burdensome procedural restrictions on cyber operations.

- Vetoed the FY21 National Defense Authorization Act, which failed to protect our national security, disrespected the history of our veterans and military, and contradicted our efforts to put America first.

Defeated terrorists, held leaders accountable for malign actions, and bolstered peace around the world.

- Defeated 100 percent of ISIS' territorial caliphate in Iraq and Syria.

- Freed nearly 8 million civilians from ISIS' bloodthirsty control, and liberated Mosul, Raqqa, and the final ISIS foothold of Baghuz.

- Killed the leader of ISIS, Abu Bakr al-Baghdadi, and eliminated the world's top terrorist, Qasem Soleimani.

- Created the Terrorist Financing Targeting Center (TFTC) in partnership between the United States and its Gulf partners to combat extremist ideology and threats, and target terrorist financial networks, including over 60 terrorist individuals and entities spanning the globe.

- Twice took decisive military action against the Assad regime in Syria for the barbaric use of chemical weapons against innocent civilians, including a successful 59 Tomahawk cruise missiles strike.

- Authorized sanctions against bad actors tied to Syria's chemical weapons program.

- Negotiated an extended ceasefire with Turkey in northeast Syria.

Addressed gaps in American's defense-industrial base, providing much-needed updates to improve the safety of our country.

- Protected America's defense-industrial base, directing the first whole-of-government assessment of our manufacturing and defense supply chains since the 1950s.

- Took decisive steps to secure our information and communications technology and services supply chain, including unsafe mobile applications.

- Completed several multi-year nuclear material removal campaigns, securing over 1,000 kilograms of highly enriched uranium and significantly reducing global nuclear threats.

- Signed an executive order directing Federal agencies to work together to diminish the capability of foreign adversaries to target our critical electric infrastructure.

- Established a whole-of-government strategy addressing the threat posed by China's malign efforts targeting the United States taxpayer-funded research and development ecosystem.

- Advanced missile defense capabilities and regional alliances.

- Bolstered the ability of our allies and partners to defend themselves through the sale of aid and military equipment.

- Signed the largest arms deal ever, worth nearly $110 billion, with Saudi Arabia.

CHAPTER 14:
SERVING AND PROTECTING OUR VETERANS

Reformed the Department of Veterans Affairs (VA) to improve care, choice, and employee accountability.

- Signed and implemented the VA Mission Act, which made permanent Veterans CHOICE, revolutionized the VA community care system, and delivered quality care closer to home for Veterans.

- The number of Veterans who say they trust VA services has increased 19 percent to a record 91 percent, an all-time high.

- Offered same-day emergency mental health care at every VA medical facility, and secured $9.5 billion for mental health services in 2020.

- Signed the VA Choice and Quality Employment Act of 2017, which ensured that veterans could continue to see the doctor of their choice and wouldn't have to wait for care.

- During the Trump Administration, millions of veterans have been able to choose a private doctor in their communities.

- Expanded Veterans' ability to access telehealth services, including through the "Anywhere to Anywhere" VA healthcare initiative leading to a 1000 percent increase in usage during COVID-19.

- Signed the Veterans Affairs Accountability and Whistleblower Protection Act and removed thousands of VA workers who failed to give our Vets the care they have so richly deserve.

- Signed the Veterans Appeals Improvement and Modernization Act of 2017 and improved the efficiency of the VA, setting record numbers of appeals decisions.

- Modernized medical records to begin a seamless transition from the Department of Defense to the VA.

- Launched a new tool that provides Veterans with online access to average wait times and quality-of-care data.

- The promised White House VA Hotline has fielded hundreds of thousands of calls.

- Formed the PREVENTS Task Force to fight the tragedy of

Veteran suicide.

Decreased veteran homelessness, improved education benefits, and achieved record-low veteran unemployment.

- Signed and implemented the Forever GI Bill, allowing Veterans to use their benefits to get an education at any point in their lives.

- Eliminated every penny of Federal student loan debt owed by American veterans who are completely and permanently disabled.

- Compared to 2009, 49 percent fewer veterans experienced homelessness nationwide during 2019.

- Signed and implemented the HAVEN Act to ensure that Veterans who've declared bankruptcy don't lose their disability payments.

- Helped hundreds of thousands of military service members make the transition from the military to the civilian workforce, and developed programs to support the employment of military spouses.

- Placed nearly 40,000 homeless veterans into employment through the Homeless Veterans Reintegration Program.

- Placed over 600,000 veterans into employment through American Job Center services.

- Enrolled over 500,000 transitioning service members in over 20,000 Department of Labor employment workshops.

- Signed an executive order to help Veterans transition seamlessly into the United States Merchant Marine.

CHAPTER 15: MAKING COMMUNITIES SAFER

Signed into law landmark criminal justice reform.

- Signed the bipartisan First Step Act into law, the first landmark criminal justice reform legislation ever passed to reduce recidivism and help former inmates successfully rejoin society.

- Promoted second chance hiring to give former inmates the opportunity to live crime-free lives and find meaningful employment.

- Launched a new "Ready to Work" initiative to help connect employers directly with former prisoners.

- Awarded $2.2 million to states to expand the use of fidelity bonds, which underwrite companies that hire former prisoners.

- Reversed decades-old ban on Second Chance Pell programs to provide postsecondary education to individuals who are incarcerated expand their skills and better succeed in the workforce upon re-entry.

- Awarded over $333 million in Department of Labor grants to nonprofits and local and state governments for reentry projects focused on career development services for justice-involved youth and adults who were formerly incarcerated.

Unprecedented support for law-enforcement.

- In 2019, violent crime fell for the third consecutive year.

- Since 2016, the violent crime rate has declined over 5 percent and the murder rate has decreased by over 7 percent.

- Launched Operation Legend to combat a surge of violent crime in cities, resulting in more than 5,500 arrests.

- Deployed the National Guard and Federal law enforcement to Kenosha to stop violence and restore public safety.

- Provided $1 million to Kenosha law enforcement, nearly $4 million to support small businesses in Kenosha, and provided over $41 million to support law enforcement to the state of Wisconsin.

- Deployed Federal agents to save the courthouse in Portland from rioters.

- Signed an executive order outlining ten-year prison sentences for destroying Federal property and monuments.

- Directed the Department of Justice (DOJ) to investigate and prosecute Federal offenses related to ongoing violence.

- DOJ provided nearly $400 million for new law enforcement hiring.

- Endorsed by the 355,000 members of the Fraternal Order of Police.

- Revitalized Project Safe Neighborhoods, which brings together Federal, state, local, and tribal law enforcement officials to develop solutions to violent crime.

- Improved first-responder communications by deploying the FirstNet National Public Safety Broadband Network, which serves more than 12,000 public safety agencies across the Nation.

- Established a new commission to evaluate best practices for recruiting, training, and supporting law enforcement officers.

- Signed the Safe Policing for Safe Communities executive order to incentive local police department reforms in line with law and order.

- Made hundreds of millions of dollars' worth of surplus military equipment available to local law enforcement.

- Signed an executive order to help prevent violence against law enforcement officers.

- Secured permanent funding for the 9/11 Victim Compensation Fund for first responders.

Implemented strong measures to stem hate crimes, gun violence, and human trafficking.

- Signed an executive order making clear that Title VI of the Civil Rights Act of 1964 applies to discrimination rooted in anti-Semitism.

- Launched a centralized website to educate the public about hate crimes and encourage reporting.

- Signed the Fix NICS Act to keep guns out of the hands of dangerous criminals.

- Signed the STOP School Violence Act and created a Commission on School Safety to examine ways to make our schools safer.

- Launched the Foster Youth to Independence initiative to prevent and end homelessness among young adults under the age of 25 who are in, or have recently left, the foster care system.

- Signed the Trafficking Victims Protection Reauthorization Act, which tightened criteria for whether countries are meeting standards for eliminating trafficking.

- Established a task force to help combat the tragedy of missing or murdered Native American women and girls.

- Prioritized fighting for the voiceless and ending the scourge of human trafficking across the Nation, through a whole of government back by legislation, executive action, and engagement with key industries.

- Created the first-ever White House position focused solely on combating human trafficking.

CHAPTER 16: CHERISHING LIFE AND RELIGIOUS LIBERTY

Steadfastly supported the sanctity of every human life and worked tirelessly to prevent government funding of abortion.

- Reinstated and expanded the Mexico City Policy, ensuring that taxpayer money is not used to fund abortion globally.

- Issued a rule preventing Title X taxpayer funding from subsiding the abortion industry.

- Supported legislation to end late-term abortions.

- Cut all funding to the United Nations population fund due to the fund's support for coercive abortion and forced sterilization.

- Signed legislation overturning the previous administration's regulation that prohibited states from defunding abortion facilities as part of their family planning programs.

- Fully enforced the requirement that taxpayer dollars do not support abortion coverage in Obamacare exchange plans.

- Stopped the Federal funding of fetal tissue research.

- Worked to protect healthcare entities and individuals' conscience rights – ensuring that no medical professional is forced to participate in an abortion in violation of their beliefs.

- Issued an executive order reinforcing requirement that all hospitals in the United States provide medical treatment or an emergency transfer for infants who are in need of emergency medical care—regardless of prematurity or disability.

- Led a coalition of countries to sign the Geneva Consensus Declaration, declaring that there is no international right to abortion and committing to protecting women's health.

- First president in history to attend the March for Life.

Stood up for religious liberty in the United States and around the world.

- Protected the conscience rights of doctors, nurses, teachers, and groups like the Little Sisters of the Poor.

- First president to convene a meeting at the United Nations to end religious persecution.

- Established the White House Faith and Opportunity Initiative.

- Stopped the Johnson Amendment from interfering with pastors' right to speak their minds.

- Reversed the previous administration's policy that prevented the government from providing disaster relief to religious organizations.

- Protected faith-based adoption and foster care providers, ensuring they can continue to serve their communities while following the teachings of their faith.

- Reduced burdensome barriers to ensure Native Americans are free to keep spiritually and culturally significant eagle feathers found on their tribal lands.

- Took action to ensure Federal employees can take paid time off work to observe religious holy days.

- Signed legislation to assist religious and ethnic groups targeted by ISIS for mass murder and genocide in Syria and Iraq.

- Directed American assistance toward persecuted communities, including through faith-based programs.

- Launched the International Religious Freedom Alliance – the first-ever alliance devoted to confronting religious persecution around the world.

- Appointed a Special Envoy to monitor and combat anti-Semitism.

- Imposed restrictions on certain Chinese officials, internal security units, and companies for their complicity in the persecution of Uighur Muslims in Xinjiang.

- Issued an executive order to protect and promote religious freedom around the world.

CHAPTER 17:
SAFEGUARDING THE ENVIRONMENT

Took strong action to protect the environment and ensure clean air and clean water.

- Took action to protect vulnerable Americans from being exposed to lead and copper in drinking water and finalized a rule protecting children from lead-based paint hazards.

- Invested over $38 billion in clean water infrastructure.

- In 2019, America achieved the largest decline in carbon emissions of any country on earth. Since withdrawing from the Paris Climate Accord, the United States has reduced carbon emissions more than any nation.

- American levels of particulate matter – one of the main measures of air pollution – are approximately five times lower than the global average.

- Between 2017 and 2019, the air became 7 percent cleaner – indicated by a steep drop in the combined emissions of criteria pollutants.

- Led the world in greenhouse gas emissions reductions, having cut energy-related CO_2 emissions by 12 percent from 2005 to 2018 while the rest of the world increased emissions by 24 percent.

- In FY 2019 the Environmental Protection Agency (EPA) cleaned up more major pollution sites than any year in nearly two decades.

- The EPA delivered $300 million in Brownfields grants directly to communities most in need including investment in 118 Opportunity Zones.

- Placed a moratorium on offshore drilling off the coasts of Georgia, North Carolina, South Carolina, and Florida.

- Restored public access to Federal land at Bears Ears National Monument and Grand Staircase-Escalante National Monument.

- Recovered more endangered or threatened species than any other administration in its first term.

Secured agreements and signed legislation to protect the environment and preserve our Nation's abundant national resources.

- The USMCA guarantees the strongest environmental protections of any trade agreement in history.

- Signed the Save Our Seas Act to protect our environment

from foreign nations that litter our oceans with debris and developed the first-ever Federal strategic plan to address marine litter.

- Signed the Great American Outdoors Act, securing the single largest investment in America's National Parks and public lands in history.

- Signed the largest public lands legislation in a decade, designating 1.3 million new acres of wilderness.

- Signed a historic executive order promoting much more active forest management to prevent catastrophic wildfires.

- Opened and expanded access to over 4 million acres of public lands for hunting and fishing.

- Joined the One Trillion Trees Initiative to plant, conserve, and restore trees in America and around the world.

- Delivered infrastructure upgrades and investments for numerous projects, including over half a billion dollars to fix the Herbert Hoover Dike and expanding funding for Everglades restoration by 55 percent.

CHAPTER 18:
EXPANDING EDUCATIONAL OPPORTUNITY

Fought tirelessly to give every American access to the best possible education.

- The Tax Cuts and Jobs Act expanded School Choice, allowing parents to use up to $10,000 from a 529 education savings account to cover K-12 tuition costs at the public, private, or religious school of their choice.

- Launched a new pro-American lesson plan for students

called the 1776 Commission to promote patriotic education.

- Prohibited the teaching of Critical Race Theory in the Federal government.

- Established the National Garden of American Heroes, a vast outdoor park that will feature the statues of the greatest Americans to ever live.

- Called on Congress to pass the Education Freedom Scholarships and Opportunity Act to expand education options for 1 million students of all economic backgrounds.

- Signed legislation reauthorizing the D.C. Opportunity Scholarship program.

- Issued updated guidance making clear that the First Amendment right to Free Exercise of Religion does not end at the door to a public school.

Took action to promote technical education.

- Signed into law the Strengthening Career and Technical Education for the 21st Century Act, which provides over 13 million students with high-quality vocational education and extends more than $1.3 billion each year to states for critical workforce development programs.

- Signed the INSPIRE Act which encouraged NASA to have more women and girls participate in STEM and seek careers in aerospace.

- Allocated no less than $200 million each year in grants to prioritize women and minorities in STEM and computer science education.

Drastically reformed and modernized our educational system to restore local control and

promote fairness.

- Restored state and local control of education by faithfully implementing the Every Student Succeeds Act.

- Signed an executive order that ensures public universities protect First Amendment rights or they will risk losing funding, addresses student debt by requiring colleges to share a portion of the financial risk, and increases transparency by requiring universities to disclose information about the value of potential educational programs.

- Issued a rule strengthening Title IX protections for survivors of sexual misconduct in schools, and that – for the first time in history – codifies that sexual harassment is prohibited under Title IX.

- Negotiated historic bipartisan agreement on new higher education rules to increase innovation and lower costs by reforming accreditation, state authorization, distance education, competency-based education, credit hour, religious liberty, and TEACH Grants.

Prioritized support for Historically Black Colleges and Universities.

- Moved the Federal Historically Black Colleges and Universities (HBCU) Initiative back to the White House.

- Signed into law the FUTURE Act, making permanent $255 million in annual funding for HBCUs and increasing funding for the Federal Pell Grant program.

- Signed legislation that included more than $100 million for scholarships, research, and centers of excellence at HBCU land-grant institutions.

- Fully forgave $322 million in disaster loans to four HBCUs in 2018, so they could fully focus on educating their students.

- Enabled faith-based HBCUs to enjoy equal access to Federal support.

CHAPTER 19:
COMBATTING THE OPIOID CRISIS

Brought unprecedented attention and support to combat the opioid crisis.

- Declared the opioid crisis a nationwide public health emergency.

- Secured a record $6 billion in new funding to combat the opioid epidemic.

- Signed the SUPPORT for Patients and Communities Act, the largest-ever legislative effort to address a drug crisis in our Nation's history.

- Launched the Initiative to Stop Opioid Abuse and Reduce Drug Supply and Demand in order to confront the many causes fueling the drug crisis.

- The Department of Health and Human Services (HHS) awarded a record $9 billion in grants to expand access to prevention, treatment, and recovery services to States and local communities.

- Passed the CRIB Act, allowing Medicaid to help mothers and their babies who are born physically dependent on opioids by covering their care in residential pediatric recovery facilities.

- Distributed $1 billion in grants for addiction prevention and treatment.

- Announced a Safer Prescriber Plan that seeks to decrease the amount of opioids prescriptions filled in America by one third within three years.

- Reduced the total amount of opioids prescriptions filled in America.

- Expanded access to medication-assisted treatment and life-saving Naloxone.

- Launched FindTreatment.gov, a tool to find help for substance abuse.

- Drug overdose deaths fell nationwide in 2018 for the first time in nearly three decades.

- Launched the Drug-Impaired Driving Initiative to work with local law enforcement and the driving public at large to increase awareness.

- Launched a nationwide public ad campaign on youth opioid abuse that reached 58 percent of young adults in America.

- Since 2016, there has been a nearly 40 percent increase

in the number of Americans receiving medication-assisted treatment.

- Approved 29 state Medicaid demonstrations to improve access to opioid use disorder treatment, including new flexibility to cover inpatient and residential treatment.

- Approved nearly $200 million in grants to address the opioid crisis in severely affected communities and to reintegrate workers in recovery back into the workforce.

Took action to seize illegal drugs and punish those preying on innocent Americans.

- In FY 2019, ICE HSI seized 12,466 pounds of opioids including 3,688 pounds of fentanyl, an increase of 35 percent from FY 2018.

- Seized tens of thousands of kilograms of heroin and thousands of kilograms of fentanyl since 2017.

- The Department of Justice (DOJ) prosecuted more fentanyl traffickers than ever before, dismantled 3,000 drug trafficking organizations, and seized enough fentanyl to kill 105,000 Americans.

- DOJ charged more than 65 defendants collectively responsible for distributing over 45 million opioid pills.

- Brought kingpin designations against traffickers operating in China, India, Mexico, and more who have played a role in the epidemic in America.

- Indicted major Chinese drug traffickers for distributing fentanyl in the U.S for the first time ever, and convinced China to enact strict regulations to control the production and sale of fentanyl.

www.ingramcontent.com/pod-product-compliance
Lightning Source LLC
Chambersburg PA
CBHW050818250726

48653CB00006B/2287